DANCING
THE
FAULT

DANCING
THE
FAULT

poems by

Judith Minty

University of Central Florida Press
Contemporary Poetry Series
Orlando

Copyright 1991 by the Board of Regents
of the State of Florida
Printed in the U.S.A. on acid-free paper ∞

Library of Congress Cataloging-in-Publication Data

Minty, Judith, 1937-
Dancing the fault / Judith Minty.
p.   cm. — (Contemporary poetry series)
ISBN 0-8130-1079-9 (cloth). — ISBN 0-8130-1080-2 (paper)
I. Title. II. Series: Contemporary poetry series (Orlando, Fla.)
PS3563.I48D3   1991
811'.54—dc20   91-4459
CIP

University Presses of Florida is the central agency for scholarly
publishing of the State of Florida's university system, producing books
selected for publication by the faculty editorial committees of Florida's
nine public universities. Orders for books published by all member
presses should be addressed to University Presses of Florida, 15 NW
15th Street, Gainesville, Florida 32611.

for Lora, Reed, and Ann

Acknowledgments

Some of these poems first appeared in:

Five Fingers Review: "Raining All Across the Country"
Green River Review: "Celebrating the Mass"
Hawaii Review: "Country Road in October," "Orchids"
Indiana Review: "Small Deaths"
Iowa Review: "Meditation on Friendship: Getting Lost in the
    Woods with Deena"
Kayak: "From the Underworld"
Ocooch Mountain News: "The Cottage Poems: Lake Michigan"
Passages North: "The Mount Pleasant Journal," "Meeting My
    Father at the River"
Pieces: "Ironing"
Poetry: "The Gray Whale"
The Small Towner: "Letter About the End of All Flesh from
    California to the Snow Country"
Woman Poet: The Midwest: Women in Literature, 1986, "Trying
    to Remember," "Christine, On Her Way to China," "Hawk,"
    "A Sense of Place," "Six Poems for Nine Crows"

"Letters to My Daughters" appeared in the chapbook *Letters to
My Daughters*, Mayapple Press, 1980.

The words by James Wright are from *Collected Prose* (University
of Michigan Press); those by Mary Elsie Robertson are from her
short story "First Snow." Walt Whitman's lines are from "Song of
Myself."

The author wishes to thank the Yaddo Corporation for providing sanctuary so that many of these poems could be written and the Michigan Council for the Arts for support and funds from the State of Michigan and the Michigan Council for the Arts so that this project could be completed. Thanks also to Dan Gerber, James D. Houston, Robert VanderMolen, and Diane Wakoski for their support and encouragement.

Cover art is *Sometimes a Woman Knows Joy*, a lithograph by Pat Custer Denison.

Photograph of the author by Robert Turney.

CONTENTS

I

II

III

DANCING
THE
FAULT

I

Missing me one place search another,
I stop somewhere waiting for you.
                                    —Walt Whitman

Meeting My Father at the River

On this evening path from camp
to river's bend, shadows
roll over and lie down in hollows,
then rise from rotting stumps
to drift along the lowland.
They stalk my boots' dull thud, branches
opening, closing overhead.
The cabin's lamp, the glowing stove,
burn behind me now in memory.

At the river, my father
still stands in light.
This will be his last trip to these waters.
His arm lifts, his line wavers,
settles over the pool.
I have often dreamed this motion:
me watching from the bank, him casting,
the whir of reel, the bend and dip of rod and arm.
Now a small trout rises to the fly.

He calls, "I got one!"
It surfaces, flickering in wetness.
He is pleased I am here to witness
and leans with grace in hip boots
for the ritual of netting,
stepping sure as a young man again.
"Good one," I cry, and wave.
He wades slowly out of sight
around the bend, creel bumping at his side.

From the Underworld

"Bats tangle in your hair," she apologizes,
hands stammering. A shiver
of wings darkens the room.

*

He chased it with a broom. She cowered
in their bed, head buried.
A faint sound: I don't know
if it was a woman's voice calling.

*

Preposterous vision: Her arm casting
over the stream, the rod
quivering, no fly. Plastic
rainbonnet tied under her chin, her dark
curls beneath the transparency.

*

The boat becalmed, tethered to land at Fayette.
We hiked through the ghost town
to woods, heard inchworms chewing oak leaves.

At dusk we drank coffee on the stern. They began
to fall like leaves in a wind. We thought
they were kingfishers at first, darting for mayflies.

*

They hang in the saplings
waiting for twilight.
The riverbank is full
of the harvest, these
pendants with wings.

*

This fear nearly smothers us.
I know a woman
from Guam whose lashes rest long
on her cheekbones, who dreams them
through the heat of summer nights.

*

Once, late, in a parking lot,
I heard a soft *ki, ki.*
Above the streetlight
I caught the sense of them, floating.

*

Someone spied it, cringing on top of the kitchen cupboard.
James came with a dishtowel,
made a knapsack and carried it to daylight.

He said it was a mouse-angel.
The women twittered like sparrows.

*

Sitting in the outhouse,
I felt a whisper near the patched shingle, saw
the tiny face by my shoulder, miniature hands
pulling the body through the knothole,
delicate ears, soft gray fur.

I picked up a board and beat
against the wall in a frenzy,
that space already filled with his presence.

*

I am often lonely at night.
Sometimes I think of you, your arms
folding me close,
the life we might have had.

Ironing

The pattern flows. Leaves and flowers blend, a river spinning over the cotton. It is my daughter's blouse. Green ripples under my fingers. Pink and blue blossom under the iron's steam. Tiny buds. The cement floor presses its back against the soles of my feet. The pipes gather pearls of moisture. I am a tree. I rise from the earth. I shade the ironing board. My hand passes back and forth, a branch in the wind. One sleeve, then the other.

Summer, but this basement remembers winter and holds loam to its heart. The water in these pipes wants to go underground, back to the dark. It is June, and my daughter sleeps in the heat of her dream. She is far from my belly now, on her white bed, still as a breath in the hospital wing. I have washed the blood from her blouse. Now this iron passes over a sleeve, it curls around a button. Colors intertwine, tangle. The petals blur. They bleed into leaves on the vines.

The car was thick with glass, little beads of glass, blue and yellow in the sun. The lace of slivers of glass, glistening on her skirt, under her bare feet. Glass clinging to her blouse, her skin. Glass in the upholstery, on the carpet, the dashboard. Prisms in the sun. A clink and tinkle like wind chimes when she stirred. Her hands gliding to her face. Glass glinting in her hair. Blood shining on the glass. Glass flowing, separating, as she stirred on the seat of the car.

I pass this iron over her blouse. Steam hisses. I hear her voice as she is lifted from the car. Steam rises from the flowers, the petals. The leaves. I am a tree. Her long hair matted with blood, the cut open on her scalp. My feet curl like roots on the floor. Sweat gathers on the pipes. I rustle over her blouse. Her hair unfurls on the pillow. The flowers blend, the leaves blur. My hand glides over the pattern, a river spinning. Her dream flows without sound. Steam hisses from the iron. Petals and leaves mingle pink and blue. Green. I am ironing her blouse. Only this motion is left.

Country Road in October

The willow, still green,
keeps this white house chaste.
But oh, that saffron cottage.

*

Cattails exploded,
their dignity in tatters.

*

All the corn stalks point east.

*

Red-tailed hawk
drifting
over what runs to hide
in the barren field.

*

They'll be the last to go,
those chrysanthemums
bordering that driveway.

*

This passage makes the chest ache.
It's orange
that hurts the most.

*

Apples dragging down the branches.
In the wagon, pumpkins.

*

Even the *Daily News* box,
yellow on its green stem.

*

The whole woods
in holy color.

*

I am amber
driving under the maples.

Trying to Remember

A note from my friend on this morning of the first snowfall. Slow waxing in letters exchanged, tones and contours spelled into words. Each envelope holds a mirror of feeling: two women naked in each other's eyes.

* * * * * * * * *

A month ago, close talk with this man I love, over cheese and wine at the kitchen table. Drifting to food after languorous hours of hands fluttering, spiralling cries. We are lonely already. We want to fly back to the body.

* * * * * * * * *

She carries the dark side of the moon under her shawl. I catch sun in a crystal by my window. We approach middle age together. Our words spin over trees, trill in strands, a sparrow's song. Between us, we create another woman.

* * * * * * * * *

Our fingers meet on the knife handle. Embarrassment at the collision, hands leaping away. We try to come together with words, but his coyote eyes glitter, a wolf rises up through my bones.

* * * * * * * * *

She writes what her grandmother said: If you wash your face in the first snow, you will have a beautiful complexion. Letters or books, something to hold in the hand. Her words are always a gift.

* * * * * * * * *

This good bread. We tear off chunks to eat with our cheese. He swirls wine in his mouth before swallowing it. Grandmother said we must honor bread, he tells me. You must kiss it before you eat it.

* * * * * * * *

Summer afternoon, my grandmother. Perhaps I am four or five. I am sitting on her lap. She is humming, I think. It is hot and we have nothing to do, no chores, no one to play with. We want and we do not want something.

* * * * * * * *

Walking in the woods, first snow sifting through pines, white puffs of breath, leaves under my feet slightly muffled. The ground disappears, a veil shudders over the land.

* * * * * * * *

She speaks of fire burning as her sons grow past her. I say my childhood ran away when I turned my back for a moment. She is pleased with this transformation. We change, she writes.

* * * * * * * *

Ferns along the path are still green, though they are growing white skins. The weight of the snow bows the stems to the ground. It is cold and the fronds do not move when I pass.

* * * * * * * *

When I sat on her lap, her fingers spun over my arm, her fingers traced lacy patterns on my skin. We were both half-asleep. She was humming, I think. The breath of her love on my arm.

* * * * * * * * *

The ferns, bent from such a little snow. A fallen birch across the path.

* * * * * * * * *

His hands burn, set me trembling. The room whispers and sighs with our caring.

* * * * * * * * *

I was so close to her heart then, her fingers pulsing over my arm.

* * * * * * * * *

Snow touches my cheeks, my eyelids. The birch lies on top of the snow.

* * * * * * * * *

We are waking, she says. We have only been hibernating.

* * * * * * * * *

We must honor it. His hand holds the bread to his lips.

* * * * * * * * *

Snow keeps falling. My tracks must be covered by now.

* * * * * * * * *

I am trying to remember what my grandmother told me.

Orchids

1

Service for townsman, old sailor
whose face I barely recall, except
as it raised
to catch telltales on the jib.

I rise with incense and candle flame
to alleluias rolling in waves.
A long time, Father,
since I faced
linen touched to chalice, the breaking of wafer.
I can't help
the hand-stitch at my breast, this genuflection.

2

We float like dreams in our funeral clothes, third car
behind the hearse, this time the uncle
who was mean and crotchety,
surgeon whose fingers finally
twisted so crooked he couldn't hold his cigar,
who never shut off the television
and let conversation fall to his wife.

Past elms, old houses
turned into offices, past storefronts blinking OPEN,
past the Black man on Peck Street,
hat over chest, standing
with head bowed until we all roll past.

3

Up North near Cross Village
in the divided cemetery, I step over
a wire fence
to low graves and bend to Chippewa names.
This is the paupers' side.

When the earth goes soft, falls
under my feet,
I think I will sink down to them,
except for the crow that shrieks,
beating wings under my ribs.

4

They roll the drawer shut on her
and I hear a woman
crying. The voice is glass shattering
on the mausoleum floor.

My chair scrapes. I stand
like stone for this suicide. My daughter
unfurls inside my belly
to take hold of her aunt's name.

5

My own aunt saw her dead mother once
in a moth
battering its wings against the kitchen door.

Last year, when her heart stopped in California, she found me
sleeping in a hotel room in Michigan.
In the dream, we held hands. Her pulse
trembled against my thumb.

6

There is no end to this, reader.
My friend was a warrior, yet even she quit.

I sat with her before she left,
but we couldn't make the journey together. Her breath
was fragile as an orchid's petal.
She was already floating in air.

Celebrating the Mass

In this hospital room, lacking the hands
of a nurse, I braid my daughter's hair
into cornrows. She is nineteen now.
When did I stop touching my child?
We have eaten sandwiches brought in and picked
at food on her tray, then turned to the mirror.
Helpless in these weeks of testing, waiting,
we want to alter her life in some way.

I think of those other mothers who have done this,
their backs aching, their hands tightening.
I think of them standing long hours
on porches of farm shacks maybe, or in tenement rooms.
I think of them weaving dark strands
to make their daughters beautiful
after the meals were served, after
the mending, the washing hung, the fields hoed.

Here, a comb sets our boundaries.
Fingers separate and part, we begin
another row: blond hair lifted, pulled,
the pattern worked in. I sculpt to the shape of bone.
Now six braids done. Now an hour. Now nineteen years.
We learn each other again. Hands to head,
fingers knitting a cap, we begin
at the temple, around the ear, crown to nape.

Easter Saturday

All morning they rose, the wild
brook trout, the pond waking
after winter. We watched them
drift below the surface, brown
shadows over moss—his voice, his arm
guiding so I could see too.

*

I sat on shore while he fished. Wind
skimmed the water like a hand passing.
Cast of the line, loop and trail,
his wrist deftly working the fly—
he gives himself to the motion.
Again. Whir of reel, breath on the surface,
silver flutter of trout in the air.
Two herons on the wing, pines
against sky, repeated again in the water.

*

Before I cooked them, I held them
cold in my hand, the slender curve
of their bodies. I felt the slick
skin, saw the iridescent circles,
red and blue flecks—
the spirit still there, moving.

Purple Finches

They come in the morning. Even before she is awake, she hears the tap-tap of their beaks, a scratching, faint whistles in the air. When sun drifts along the bed, she floats to the surface.

They ripple over the feeder. The males flame in the light, their pink and rose feathers. The females are delicate, softer. She wants to say, "Look, they are beautiful," but there is no one. They fly up and wait in the pines, then sink back.

The window mutes their voices. She circles the room slowly so she won't startle them. They bend to the seeds and crack them with their beaks. They were not here yesterday or the day before. They will not come tomorrow. She puts her fingers to the glass and enters their rhythm. She steps inside their color.

Snow in April

Warm days for a week,
overcoats shoved to the back
of the closet and windows open,
the gas turned down.

Yesterday, warnings of other false hopes
from men in shirtsleeves at the shop,
mothers softly at the dinner table.
Sons and daughters act smug,
say that Winter's given up.
They boast that a day's drive south
forsythia and crocus explode with color.

But the old ones are restless.
They tell the tales over again,
even as the ground turns white
and lonely arms of coats
stretch out from their hangers.

II

LETTERS
TO MY
DAUGHTERS

Letters to My Daughters

1

Your great-grandfather dreamed that his son
would be an engineer, the old man,
the blacksmith with square hands.
To the Finns up north in that snow country
engineer was like doctor today. In the forties
in Detroit, I learned to play the violin.
So did my father when he was a boy in Ishpeming.
He and I never spoke about becoming. Our conversation
was my bow slipping over the strings, my fingers
searching for notes to tell him, his foot tapping time.
That violin cracked ten years ago, it dried out
from loneliness in the coat closet.
Your grandfather, the engineer, sometimes plays his
at night behind a closed kitchen door.
Your grandmother sews and turns up the television.
But what of you two? The piano you practiced over
is still here, a deaf-mute in our living room.
I strike an imperfect chord now and remember
we never spoke of dreams.

2

Once, in Geneva, I saw gypsies. Four of them.
Ravens wearing hats like sombreros.
I stopped still on the sidewalk, was caught by their fire.
I wanted to follow their shadows, drink wine with them.
I wanted to laugh with them, dance with them,
learn all their songs. But your father
touched my arm, told me to speak French
to the policeman, ask directions to our hotel.
Yesterday, Cynthia read a poem about gypsies, how they steal
small children. You were both in Michigan then,
I seldom thought of you on that trip.
She says that her husband laughs, does not believe her
when she whispers how the gypsies came,
flashing their eyes, strolling across the Iowa cornfields.
Listen, you two. If you ever see one in a strange city,
follow him. Think of that fire
he keeps, his house full of urchins.
Those men in Switzerland, they never looked at me.

3

It's a joke in this family, more yours
than mine, that I still think of myself as young.
I am still the child, and the house on Northlawn,
torn down for an expressway, is here in another town.
The glider still creaks when I shell peas for dinner,
the rock garden blooms primroses by the steps,
yellow clapboard flashes inside my eye.
But somewhere in twenty-five years
I have lost the front door. Not the reflection.
Walking down Puritan or Wyoming, a girl
of twelve, or fourteen, lopes out of store windows.
Bony wrists, small breasts and hips, neck thrust forward.
You are never in that image. Beyond perhaps.
Now I grow fat and my eyes are wrong, I often
turn away from the mirror. I can't
find her these days, except in a belly that churns
when I hear about the Chicago artist
who ties up young girls and films them
as they are raped, slashed, sodomized, burned.

4
When I was five or six, I filled my fists
with pansies, velvet yellows and purples
from the neighbor's garden. I meant them for my mother,
somehow to honor the memory of her hands, the smell
of her, those breasts I had aged from.
When I thrust them at her, she frowned and led me back
up the street, my hand still a tight vase.
I cried on Mrs. Bunting's steps, next to her rock garden,
and told her I was sorry. What I meant was
my mother never smelled the flowers or put them into water.
Last spring you, the eldest, brought me
a yellow violet you found while walking home.
Four lemon petals brushed with purple in my palm.
You said, "Look. Such a small thing. And perfect."
I lifted it to my face, then on impulse ate it.
We both laughed, but I still taste the tartness.
Now you, the youngest, return with a bouquet of daisies.
They have no scent, I know, but I hold them
to my nose, then pour a pitcher of water,
and never ask you where you picked them.

5

This morning, I laze in bed, gathering news
from *The Free Press*. Our tomcat is an old man,
camped under the tent of the sheets.
He would like to sleep here all day.
Even the younger cats have stopped hunting. Those two
prefer sunshine through the window now.
Outside, they flutter their paws over icy sidewalks
and shiver like wounded robins for the heater.
The labrador's muzzle has bleached white
from seasons of ruffling ducks out of marsh grass.
Her eyes weep and she groans and wheezes,
I must lift her when she scrambles up the stairs.
It is you who named them all, child's block letters
into words that we pulled from a wool hat.
Softy, Frisky, Tar. Uncle Sam for the Fourth of July.
Strange, that in this winter season
one of you has called me by my first name.

6

One gone, the other still here, the two of you
split like Siamese twins must be,
the empty space never to fill completely,
although the other branches out with this pruning.
You, the elder, wanted roots far away
as an ocean. I knew about that
and drove you there, helped you transplant
among men who rhyme. Their language
was a cage to me, but you
were starving for that plotted soil.
"No more wilderness," you cried. "Dead," I said.
No. Not daughter, but mother.
When I left you, I thought of Paris and the guillotine,
of how the accused knows but perhaps never feels
pain until the blade falls. Alone in the car
heading west, I studied against truck lights
my arm, the place where the hand had been.

7

This week I received two love letters,
one from a boy still in high school, another
from an older man in his twenties,
a man who whispers about mountains.
Your father doesn't read my mail. He pretends
disinterest in the postmarks, the crimped penmanship,
the shy poems folded inside.
Even when it mattered, he never wrote me. I think he was
embarrassed by misspelled words, stammering lines.
But now he watches me as I watch
for the mailman's truck. He notices
how my fingers stain the curtains when I part them,
that I float through snow in my bathrobe to the mailbox.
I hide the letters in dark drawers and pull them out
when I can't remember my name. They smell like wild violets.
Your father? Lately, I find him bent at his desk,
hands knotted over blank paper. I must tell him
those young men are only in love with poetry.

8

Summer, and you two here. Boarders
who sleep till noon while I take your messages
and wash your empty glasses and stack your clothes
and mutter and scratch for time at my desk.
This spring, while you were in school, I imagined
we were like the robins outside our kitchen window.
Each day I stood at the sink, the nest
so close I could have cradled it in my palm.
When it rained, the mother spread her wings like an awning.
She never left. The father
brought worms to her until the babies hatched.
Then she bustled back and forth, a dozen trips a day,
to fill their gaping mouths, to carry off their excrement.
The third week she flew away. They cried all day for her,
but the next morning those fledglings had disappeared.
In the nest, still, is a splash of blue,
the beautiful egg that never opened.

9

When I was thirteen, my mother
called the pound to take Patsy away. The dog
was old, a tumor big as a baseball bobbled from her neck.
It was Saturday, I'd been to the movies,
seen Captain Marvel save a whole city.
The truck was pulling away from Northlawn
as I turned the corner. I felt the loss then,
ran home screaming, blaming my mother.
When he was a boy, your father
watched his dog try to jump on a snowbank
out of ruts made by cars. The milkman never saw Fuzzy.
The only witness: a boy who called too late.
Now Softy, with her fur for your faces,
her purrs singing at your ankles, is gone.
Real grief drives by sometimes on a sunny day
to corner us. Blame me,
blame anyone if it helps.
This taste of dying is hard to swallow alone.

10

Even though the plants are only a foot tall,
you, our sixteen-year-old baby, dream them ripe
with fruit, the tomatoes scarlet in their fullness.
And you come flushed from sleep to tell this wealth,
how each night you root through rich soil
to reap the harvest of your first garden.
Nineteen years ago we dreamed your sister,
the child not of our own mating, although we tried,
who came to us, all rosy, at seven weeks
and slept cribbed in the room below ours.
Three times in those first days
we woke at night, eyes blind like moles
against the lamplight, and groped the sheets,
palms flailing in the empty air between us.
We meant to find her when she cried, to make
her in that space of barren bed
our child, the fruit of love and holding,
before we opened to each other and the space
between us suddenly remembered empty, before we fled
the stairs and soothed the dream
and counted soil for what it was
and took the harvest and felt lucky.

11

Lunching with you at a restaurant on Commonwealth Ave.
in this alien city of subways and accents,
I smile at your dark hair curling to escape the rain
and half-listen to two law students on my left. They are
closer to me than you, cutting your sandwich across the table;
I could touch the arm of the necktied young man
next to me, if I wanted. In this crowded place
all conversations blend. "In the case
of Jacobitz vs. Muller . . ." I ask if you need money;
you shake your head and fine wisps lift in the motion.
"Professor Hewitt said we should pay particular attention . . ."
I speak of the woods I just left, but your eyes wander.
She will marry one of these Boston men, I think, as I watch
my neighbor, holding his fork in midair, still talking the Bar.
Their hands, I want to tell you. Beware of hands
too pale and soft. These hands have forgotten
the bark of trees. They have never sanded wood to its skin,
never felt rope slide across the palm. These fingers
have never reached into the earth, never touched
the heart of a deer. How can I tell you my fear for children
born of these men, children with vestigial arms,
two fingers to hold a fork, a pen, nothing more.

12

Spring, and you worry at the bee tree again.
Blond, nearly as tall as I now, you brood
up through the unfolding leaves.
Three years they have swarmed, clustered
thick at the mouth of this maple. Now you wait
for them to hum awake in their cradle,
to leave their long trunk of sweetness.
Three summers the beeline has whirred
above your head to dogwood, to lilac, to pear tree,
the neighbor's flower bed. Now, Spring again,
everything in bud, we watch the entrance
for the exit of the harem, for new drones
who live to die for their queen. You insist
she has flown, that this time it is the end of honey.
A week you have waited, and still I am
unable to tell you how a woman can love
more than one man, as I stand beside you,
as the two of us hover at this hive.

13

" . . . and when the snows came and everything froze
they slunk close to the back door,
snarling, teeth flashing in moonlight . . ."
It is a father's story of wolves, repeated
nights for his weak, city children
until we grew strong and owned those winters,
blue ice sliding from his eyes to ours
(they did not know what to do, those Finns,
huddled close to the wood stove,
coffee steaming, a draft circling their feet).
" . . . and snow drifted around the house,
packed in waves high as the bedroom windows,
and their howls rose from the sea of it . . ."
Listen, you two, put your heads
close to mine: blond and dark, then darker.
I want to tell you a mother's story, about sounds
that come in the night, about footprints circling a house.
We never know how to send it away
so we take it in, in here, into this body, this cage.
And when the fire dwindles, when the door flies open,
we rush toward the moon. Fur bristling on our shoulders,
we send shrill cries out through the night.

14

Even in this bright time for women, you will pass
much of your lives in the kitchen. At last without anger,
that no longer seems wrong to me.
There is pleasure in cooking as well as in eating,
and this room, full of good smells and the oven's heat,
sings with the warmth of our making.
Three tall women now, we move our hands
over stove or sink, then turn
from our chopping and stirring to tell what we know.
It is here, heads bent over steaming teacups,
that we read or write letters, here
that we watch for the mail truck.
The slow man who lives in this house knows
how we are and built us a bird feeder. Then he painted it
yellow and planted it outside our kitchen window.
This morning I sit alone at the table and watch the blizzard
boil into its fifth day. Juncos dart and dip
to the seeds, now a female cardinal shyly drops down.
Her mate, bright in the bare oak, watches over the path,
the long strides your father made through the snow.

15

I did not know then that there would come a time when
one snow would blow into the next with no clear beginning,
no clear ending.

—Mary Elsie Robertson

Winters ago, I cried for babies, wanted to swell
to bursting with the seed of lovemaking.
I dreamed through cold
of warm-hearted daughters at my breast
and swore, somehow, you would make me whole.
Now gone away, your own breasts
make ready, and I grope
through another thaw in this stranger's woods.
I search the crusted snow for a sign
of ripeness, a need to mark Spring on the equinox,
and find it finally in lowland.
In this bog, full with the odor of skunk cabbage,
I bend to touch the first blooms:
waxen blossom, shy child folded inside.
I take in the heat of growth, the perfect circles
around each flower, and feel the whole earth
pregnant under my boots, under the stubborn snow.

16

This summer holiday, your father and grandfather
drift into the yard. Hands in pockets, they rumble
in gutturals about engines or fishing—the words fall away.
Inside, everything mutes. Sunk
into the upholstery, we three
speak politely. Grandmother, mother, daughter: strangers
confused by what was and is. Hemmed between you two,
blood and bone stretch through me, so tight
that when you run a hand over your forehead
in her motion, or lean forward to speak
as she does, I make a pair of fists in my lap
to halt another imitation. This fine, precarious thread!
I remember when she knelt to comb my hair, when, forgive me,
I diapered you. The seamed face
I find in the mirror is the one you know,
not the young woman in my mind's eye.
In this straining, I grow lonely for the girl
locked inside my mother, the one you and I never met,
except in these feathery hands of ours, or how we walk
across a room, or sleep curled to the fabric of our men.

17

In this house where you blossomed to women, I sift
through the stuff of our rooms, then seal it
in cardboard boxes. Books and dishes. Linens.
The essence of home, now in cartons
halfway to the ceiling. In this leaving, I take
with me pieces of your life as well:
photographs, a misshapen squirrel one of you made
from clay, a vase that held May flowers.
I think we stayed here too long, grew too close to the form
of this place. Now it hurts to break away.
Women are sentimental. It comes from keeping
a house, the daily work we do. Beds and laundry, meals
prepared to be eaten, furniture waxed and rewaxed.
I falter under so many layers
of repetition, even as I gather, discard possessions.
We do what we have to do. In the precise labeling
I give you this to take with you:
Nothing remains as it was. If you know this, you can
begin again, with pure joy in the uprooting.

III

When the way is internalized, practice
can be continued anywhere.
                    —Zentatsu Baker-Roshi

The Cottage Poems: Lake Michigan

1. Entering

I have taken this cottage out of season.
Now it is just these two old women and me
who finish summer without ornament.
From my window I watch
them squirrel along the path,
their arms full of blankets and sheets. They will
board up another cabin today.

Once, everything was new here: rusted lawn chair,
broken grill, iron rail leaning out from its post
(Perhaps that hunchback held dark men in her arms.
Did her sister swim under the moon?).
Even inside, paint curls from the windowsill.

Behind me, the refrigerator wheezes,
the screen door bangs shut. Sand
blossoms from my feet
running down the dune to the beach.

2. The Storm

All afternoon, wrestling with words at the desk, heat
kneading the moist air. My pinned-up hair
wants to escape and my throat closes,
remembering deserts, trying to remember
how to sing. Today
even the flies are fierce as sharks,
swimming around my legs.

We are waiting for something to happen.

It begins first near the sink, a gasp of air drawn in:
pressure sinking, then rising.
When the trees shake their fists at the lake,
I cross my arms and watch from the doorway.
A flash low at the horizon, then the wind
surges in waves—a breath
on my skin, the hand passing over my forehead.

3. Monarchs

Each year they sail back, falling before the leaves.
They dip and flutter, the air full
with orange petals, to kiss the warty pods.

Outside my door, this dunefield
of milkweed and goldenrod;
bright, hairy drupes dragging down the sumac;
acorns hailing on the roof.

So many butterflies scattered on the beach.
Wings broken, they tremble against shore
like children tearing away.

4. Waves

Yesterday the lake
slept without breath, hands
still as a woman waiting.
Morning, the clouds slid over her.
Evening, the sun ran away.

Today she stirs, shakes
white froths of hair.
I feel the mood of this stretching,
this swinging of arms.

If I could, I would descend
the fragile stairs with a sail,
leap naked into the waves,
lift out over the blue skin—
I am that restless.

5. Inside

All this rain:
the cottage stands limp
under dripping eaves.
        Everything—
        curtain, rug, blanket, cushion
        —swells
with the weight of water.
Even the eyelids
heavy, and the mind
swims in the pool of it.
I pass this day
wading
from window to drizzly window.

6. Healing

Half a week spent drowning in rain.
Below, the lake calls
in its dim voice, and fog
hangs on the dune. Everything
clings, like this sand to my boots.

Enough.

All the way out to the road
stretch woods, a cave of oak and pine.
Another who suffered from rain
carved a path through them once.

Deeper,

to the center of rotting timber.
Oh chanterelle, amanita, agaricus,
glowing fruit of rain. Oh parasols,
oh hedgehogs, earthstars. Oh fairy ring,
you must be what I was looking for.

7. The Cardinal

It was the cardinal, the bright male,
who brought me out on the dune
that last evening. He was chipping
from a dead branch near the sumac,
the wind catching his tail feathers,
bending them southward so that he looked
broken and oddly comical on his perch.

There was no time to lift the glasses.
It took only four wingbeats
to clear the sumac, then the blowout,
and pass over the pines to the north.
White head and tail,
bald eagle hunting the shoreline home,
the red bird and me standing witness.

The Mount Pleasant Journal

9/22

Still this.
As I climb the apartment stairs,
I worry that the phone will ring,
stop ringing,
before I turn my key in the lock.

10/7

This morning rain drifts
to another town. Now the whole courtyard
sleeps, its moist mouth silent.
      No. A blackbird
      calls.
      Another answers
      (water beading on red shoulders).
      Now a sparrow
      cleanly fills the air and the pheasant
      echoes from pools in the cornfield.
We are all surfacing from dream,
shaking our heads,
as drops fall from the eaves
in no particular pattern.

11/15

At last, a bird at the suet cake.
Welcome sparrow, lord of my balcony,
strutting this railing,
sunflower seed in your beak.

1/16

Third day of the blizzard.
Locked up in these rooms, pacing
and calling for friends,
I end at the window again.

Once, somewhere, was land,
the before of this white sea below.
I stand watch
over an ocean of snow, over waves

that swirl or rise in peaks.
I am a stone
sinking and this building
a ship that shudders, sways,
then lumbers but makes no headway.

1/22

Sun lights a million fires
over snow, tiny crystals of water.
This bright morning blurs
all memory of storms and the heart
soars in a celebration of blue.

Skis clamped to my boots, I push out,
a heron, across the meadow.
I am light,
a feather on the surface. I cross
the field, glide and stroke. Glide again.

In this whispering, I try to remember
wings. My tracks
show where I came from, courtyard
small as a bird's eye.
Ahead still, the dark woods.

3/7

Thaw long in coming. With a roar
the roof shakes off its burden,
and in the meadow, briars
poke through the crusty snow.
This holy Tuesday
the big oak across the field
blossoms with blackbirds, singing.

3/25

When I found him in the furrow,
only a foot and wing left,
I brought him home to a bed of pine cones.
        Tonight his foot
        claws and flexes on the cave wall
        of this apartment, and his epaulets
        shine gold in the candlelight.
We see what we want to see.
I live here suspended, knowing a blackbird
takes flight now over pine trees.

Six Poems for Nine Crows

(after a painting by S. Krause in Philip Booth's apartment,
Syracuse, New York)

September now.
Only a breath of summer remains.
Uprooted, I stand at this eastern window
and watch sparrows drift from the maple
like brown leaves. I own nothing here,
the eye clear in new air.

* * * *

Owl feather, finch petal, jay leaf,
flicker branch, pheasant stem:
feathers dropped in passage. Now I
plant them near his painting of crows in a field.
        One flaps his wings
        at a newcomer, beak open
        and shrilly warning. Another
        stands guard. The rest
        tend to the harvest.
These silent relics bloom
in their vases, each vein
of color defined, barbs
still poised to the flight.

* * * *

Wherever we live, those we care about
find us, and we wait for their letters.
They glide from post office to mailbox like homing pigeons,
the heart inside pulsing "Friend."

Now this news about rifles and chain saws
ripping Mohawk trees, about SWAT teams,
about women hiding in their houses, this plea to help
a stubborn elder who tried to save the trees

makes my hands heavy.
600 miles west of here, and north,
are Chippewa woods. I'm a fool to imagine
no one has timbered that land since I left it.

* * * * *

"Philip's tree."
There, I've named it, the maple
outside my bedroom window. I know it
belongs to itself and I'm only a renter here—
still he's told me the pleasure it's given,
so these words are for him:

In this gale wind, far from the sea, your tree
flaps its wings and turns wild.
It means to lift up, soar back to its mother, back
to the shade, the dark seed of before.
I witness it all from your window.
The wind calls through a thin crack,
even this paper flutters.

* * * * *

The station begun, though I'd meant to wait
a month for the earth's shell to form.
First a gossipy jay, then a grackle in mourning.
Now today, a convention of sparrows.
The whole balcony flickers brown. They feed
like horses at a trough, queue up on the railing for turns.
The thinkers take the floor and spilled seed,
beaks opening, closing, to the glory of food.

Last week, driving in the country, the sun barely risen,
I passed a farmer in overalls, bucket heavy at his side
(He is crossing to his sheep. They nearly dance
at his coming, black faces nudging each other by the fence.).
We all tremble for something—the hand
to reach into the slop pail, a letter,
the telephone to ring—our morning nourishment.

* * * *

This place belongs to others. Stretching out
in these rooms, I sense the skin of their lives.
Walls don't keep secrets.
Each breath that seeps from our lungs
leaves a thread clinging to plaster or fabric,
a chorus of whispers humming.
The monstrous shadow rises and falls without the body,
and we long for them to join again.
In this half-light, dark wings
burst open, the maple scratches at the window.

Meditation on Friendship:
Getting Lost in the Woods with Deena
—Jamesville, New York

You think I am like your grandmother
because I've been so far
North. But even a wolf marks territory, even she
sets her teeth, lets no one beyond.

*

We stand at the edge
of winter. The desert beats in your blood.
I haven't lived here
long enough, though I tell you
I've been here before, though in fact
not exactly here. These are civilized woods.

*

You try to put on
the skin of this place, but it doesn't fit, the pelt
stretches and binds.
Oh Friend, we aren't animals after all.
We're troubled women, unable
to see clearly.

*

These are the oaks where, in October,
migrating robins rested. Now chattering half-truths,
we step off the path into mud. We know better,

still we wander a thread of a creek
to logs and dead leaves, musty soil.
We've not been touched for so long.

*

Almost dark, and we're turned
to repeating mistakes. I'm ashamed of my feet
stumbling, snapping twigs, grown clumsy as old women.
They sense the circles we've made.

*

We're lost and we know it.
There's no farmhouse, no cabin. We're locked in
these woods, the trees our markers,
the setting sun our compass.

*

We need to speak from the heart again, to listen
for the river. It's our way out, that water
flowing. We need to go
downstream to the bridge, we need
to reach the other side touching.

Meditation on Friendship:
Driving to the Baths in a Blizzard with Deena
—Saratoga Springs, New York

Once, what left our hands made birdsongs:
the voice of stones, a song like a loon's
skimming the frozen pond.
In that motion, our arms were wings.
We carried the notes inside.

*

Now another winter, and we plow our way
East again. This need
drives us back to healing water.

*

You call this cold magic, this pelting,
this blindness we enter. My hands,
tight on the wheel, want to believe.

Slush scuttles, catches our wheels,
and we're tossed to the edge, then back to the line.
In this small space of car, we turn
from each other. Distance grows

until voices of truckers float from the radio.
Men we can't see hold us steady:
is this the way it must be?

*

We used to know guides. Once we danced
in hot coals, played the drum between our legs.
Now this ache we won't speak of.

*

Those hags at the baths. They know
about women who suffer from longing.
Now they're drawing our water, steam rises up.
Now they're pouring the lotion.
Now they're heating the sheets.

When they lift us to the tables, we'll give away
these bodies. We'll take in their gnarled hands,
their snorts and their grunts. We'll let them
soak us and oil us, knead us and pound us.
They'll croon as they wrap these bones and this flesh.

*

Damned or not, we'll be clean
in our darkness. Oh Friend, we're here—
that's what matters—and we will
come out of this white time holy.

Small Deaths

Sway and flicker of leaves, sunlight
dappling the floor of the woods,
long ripple of wave.

All week this touching: Thee
and thee. Now thee.

What will we give in this parting?
Love bite on the thigh, wing of an owl,
your grandmother's hair woven into a chain,
this blue stone shaped like a heart.

Letter About the End of All Flesh
from California to the Snow Country

Oh Friend, how apart we are. Here it rains,
seven days and seven nights. Do you remember
this torrent, now in your white silence
(puff of breath, crunch and creak of boot on snow)?
Do you recall this fury
of water rising, water falling, the surge
and rush, the flow, this awful thrust?

It rains. Nothing here is white.
The ocean casts up timber in its foam
as if to toss the tree roots back to land again.
It beats at wharf and bridge
and shore. The earth gives up.
It breaks away, slides down the hills,
drags house and pine and roadway in its oozing trail.

How could you feel this in your cold
and quiet time, this rain that falls through night and day?
From the cliff, I watch
whales spouting, on their mating trip to Baja.
In the canyon, all this damp and soggy week,
an echo of someone pounding nails,
building that ship to follow them.

The Gray Whale

Before the advent of motorized sailing vessels, it is believed that certain species of whales could communicate across hemispheres.

I. Inside the Whale's Head

We climb to get there, to what seems
only rock or rubble from a distance.
My friends want to play,
but I'm new to the coast, still afraid
of what comes with the waves, undulating—
the long strands of kelp, sea palms
and weeds, whatever curls in on itself.

    It must have known it could not go back
    to fluid motion and grace, even as it
    rose from the deep, gave its bulk to the tide.
    I was inland when it beached. I didn't witness
    the passage of breath, the souvenir hunters,
    the mourners. My friends saw
    the helicopter lifting it in pieces.

No one warned me about this.
Above the sea now, it bakes in the sun
—flesh gone to the air, the rest
growing into the earth. We walk
the length of the spine in our small shoes,
we touch the stumps of its bones, we circle
the jaw, we give away our words.

    I am nothing when I stand inside its head.

Santa Cruz, California

II. The Fisherman Calling

The fisherman stands far out on the rocks.
He is past the cove and we're just two women
who haven't learned the ocean. We watch him
cast and cast again through our binoculars
—his rod glints, the rocks glisten,
waves fall and fall on each other.
This once was a whaling station. We came looking
for spouts, but find only a man fishing morning away.

When he waves his arms, we think he has fallen or is
trapped by the tide. The speck of him grows in the lens.
He waves, and we follow a path along the spine of the cliff
past allysum and poppy, foam and crash of surf.
The wind whips our hair, our feet rattle stones
—past thorn and stubble of grass—the sea
booms against the rocks as we go to save the fisherman.

When we stand above him, we still don't see.
He cups his hands and shouts, but the wind
takes his voice. Then he points to the water
below us. It rises, gray
mottled skin. It heaves its weight up.
Side and fluke. Eye. It dives and explodes again.
It grazes the rocks. Dives and rises again
—the sea churning, the wind blowing,
the four of us joined each time in the air.

                                        Davenport Landing, California

III. Following By Boat

Gale winds for a week. Now a drizzle
settles the sea, and our rented boat
throbs over the bar, out of the harbor.
Binoculars and cameras hanging from our necks,
we pretend to be experts, not eager
for bubbles, for spouts, for seabirds flying low.

    They are here, they are waiting.
    They listen to our chatter, our jokes, and our laughter.
    Their shadows drift under the hull.

    Now they rise to port, to port.
    Five giants.
    Five monsters
    spangled with barnacles.

    Now dancers leaping in unison
    —buffalo, tiger, whatever has left us—
    hill and rock, curve and sway of the universe.

From the mouth of Mad River, they touch,
to the mouth of the Eel,
past Table Bluff—they touch, they touch.
Loop and slide of the dream—rolling over and under.
Body and Drum—beside us, in front.
They touch. They sigh. They touch.

    All this we've lost.
    All this—forgotten.

Eureka, California

Hawk

Dead hawk outside my bedroom window,
even the cats won't touch it.
I laid low for three days,
didn't leave the house,
and wrote my Cherokee friend.
He hasn't answered, the hawk's
been waiting. Today I took

the tail feathers and feet.
I feel worst about the feet,
hanging from the backporch beam—
fists clenched, claws like my own hand
holding the knife. I knew
when the other one flew over, keening,
he wouldn't recognize her like that.

Jacoby Creek, California

A Sense of Place

There is a genius of place, a presence, and
because there is, people's feelings accumulate about it.
                                        —James Wright

I

I recall that California yard full of caged birds
we used to drive past on our way to the ocean
and the parrot shop at the Santa Cruz Mall, alive
with exotic feathers—we all dressed in colors then—
that woman in the red cape who wandered Mission Blvd.,
street musicians in Guatemalan shirts,
flower shops with tubs of roses by the curb.
Now I'm in snow country, still thinking
of pink and yellow buildings, of persimmons
in the market, and rhododendrons flopping off their stems.
Here, these Eastern woods have just shrugged off winter
and the trees are full of brown birds,
bright voices hiding in the branches.

II

Summers ago in Leland, I watched a swimmer
walk out of Lake Michigan, her wet hair gleaming
and her skin, with its coat of oil,
glittering in the sun. Behind her, blue
and stretching to the sky, the water sparkled.
Everything shone, even crystals of sand around our blanket.
That was the month of butterflies, thousands
of monarchs on their way to Mexico—
I don't know how they can make it so far.
Once, in California, I walked
through the eucalyptus trees at night
and heard the whisper of their wings while they slept.

III

When the bear came to me, I already knew
that trees walk at night, that the river speaks,
and the wind knows everything.
It was October, evening at the Yellow Dog. I was
reading near the stove, trying to keep warm, trying
to ignore some mice building a nest on the shelf.
Maybe he was watching all week, maybe
he just found my light—I don't know.
At first I thought his bawling and crying
were embers in the stove, then a cow,
but those Michigan woods were never farmland.
I turned down the lamp and ran to the window and saw
only my own reflection in the light from the fire.

IV

Just weeks ago, I sat on the bank
of the Smith River, up near the Oregon border.
I was mourning snow then, dreaming white hills
and wishing cold wind in the face.
Now, I'm across the country and ice
has just let loose this pond. It's May,
bass shiver up from the mud, and new leaves
reflect on the water's skin. I feel lucky
they've found me, whoever they are
that flow with the water, float on the wind.
At this moment, now, midges and darters skim the surface,
and the bass break in circles to take them.

Saratoga Springs, New York

Flying from Boston to Portland
on Christmas Eve

Somewhere, just past Minneapolis,
day quit in fading roses.
Now, in the dark, little Christmas towns
glint like constellations on the prairie.
All those farmers and widows and priests down there
don't see us lumbering westward in the belly of this plane,
our words muffled, compressed, against the partitioned
walls, ceiling. They don't know how afraid we are
of falling, of exploding, of sailing on forever.
They don't know how we long to dream our tinsel childhood.

We are so close up here, our fingertips nearly touching,
strangers encased in metal and plastic.
The man next to me is a timber broker,
he sells trees to Japan.
He is lonely, and I smile, flying over this earth.
"I'm staying in a hotel," he says
and asks for my phone number.
"Merry Christmas," he whispers and hands me a marijuana joint.
Beyond the portholes, night is black ice, no stars gleam.
Below, only candles in the windows light the way.

Raining All Across the Country

Our words, drifting back and forth over the phone wire,
testify to something: At least we can share this rain.
It marries us again, as if the Sierras, the desert, the Rockies,
the plains, the Mississippi, the Great Lakes
did not separate us—for they are also in rain.
You tell me you have lit a fire. I, also, am chilled
inside my new, thick sweater. The rain falls softly
as my morning slides into your afternoon, and your voice,
through the receiver, moves the small bones of my ear,
then flows like blood to my arms, my legs.

I want to tell you how it is with me—that I am
here in California yet also there where you are, like an inhale
and exhale, a coming and going that disturbs nothing.
I see you sitting in that green chair, the phone
to your right ear. You are fiddling with something,
a small piece of paper, rolling it into a ball.
Now you stand in front of the desk. You are watching
rain fall on the sumac, on their drenched purple crests,
on their leaves turned to burgundy, on the wet meadow,
on the heavy pine boughs by the hill—all in misty rain.

If I told you this, would you understand? For you,
my rented house is only a number on an envelope. We no longer
share a bed. Your shirts don't hang in my closet. You've never
stood at this window or sat in this borrowed rocker
looking down at this puddled street, these shiny rooftops
slanting down to the bottoms, the foggy bay beyond.
You didn't see me this rainy morning, digging holes
for the daffodil bulbs. When I set them in the earth, I was
placing myself here in spring, in the sunshine that's coming.

Arcata, California

Christine, On Her Way to China:
An Earthquake Poem

"Buy that blouse," she whispered,
the earth already moving, though we didn't know it yet.
We walked over from the car, the blouse
expensive, pulling us to the window.
We walked rich and daring, with that thrust to our hips.

The gold beads were electric; she was my friend.
The night before, when I confessed my sins,
we'd both wept for what might have been—
the dreams that never rose, the lost father of the child in us.
"Buy it," she said in her throaty Austrian way.

She'd just come from snow country to gape at fuchsias,
Scotch broom and poppies by the roadside,
to Northern California, where everything grows big and wet and
     lush.
She'd come from barren white, a nine-month winter,
to trees in leaf and rivers shimmering like snakeskins.

I saw bolts of lightning explode from the black silk;
I felt something break, a sunburst;
I heard a rustle, the crack and fall of timber.
"Aztec goddesses in temples," said Christine.
"Will you take a charge card?" I asked the saleswoman.

The plates were sliding then, the brain exposed,
a flash and spark, granite rasping granite.
The jolt came then, the earth in motion.
Buildings swayed, chimneys fell, the TV talk was rock and grind
     and rumble.
I spun glittering before the mirror and knew we danced the fault.

Christine is flying now to China.
My earthquake blouse gleams from the open closet.
Someone told me once how he'd been standing in a valley,
felt the tremble, and watched the fields roll like ocean waves.
I thought, even then, how we are planted here,
how ordinary our lives are, how we must
make adventure from these briefest shifts and passings.

Eureka, California

Photograph by Robert Turney

A native of Michigan, Judith Minty now splits her living between Michigan and northern California, where she is Professor of English and Women's Studies at Humboldt State University. Her first book, *Lake Songs and Other Fears*, was recipient of the United States Award of the International Poetry Forum in 1973. Her other books include *Yellow Dog Journal, Letters to My Daughters, In the Presence of Mothers*, and *Counting the Losses*.

UNIVERSITY OF CENTRAL FLORIDA
CONTEMPORARY POETRY SERIES